*Inside a Refugee Crisis:
My Time in South Sudan*

by Sandy Althomsons

Copyright 2014 © Sandy Althomsons

ISBN-13: 978-0-9907772-1-2

Cover art by Grace Molteni
Book design by Elias Primoff

All proceeds from sales of this book will be donated to
Doctors Without Borders/Médecins Sans Frontières (MSF)

This book is dedicated to all the national staff of MSF, past and present, around the world.

Foreword

Shortly after South Sudan gained independence in July 2011, armed violence broke out in Sudan's Blue Nile state.

Within a year, over 100,000 people left their homes and crossed the border into Maban County, South Sudan. Many refugee camps were quickly set up before the start of the rainy season. Crowding, flooding, and unsanitary conditions set the stage for a communicable disease outbreak.

The first deaths were reported in July 2012; two pregnant women and one child, all with yellow eyes. Soon, many more patients were admitted to the Doctors Without Borders/Médecins Sans Frontières (MSF) hospital. Hepatitis E virus was confirmed in all of the camps.

MSF began scaling up their mission, bringing in more international staff, including doctors, nurses, and epidemiologists. I arrived in June 2013, just after the peak. The following are the messages I sent home, and photographs I've compiled from others who were on mission with me.

—Sandy Althomsons, 2014

June 1, 2013

I was up until 2:00AM last night downloading stuff onto a USB key. I decided not to take my laptop or mini-tablet when Kate, my HR rep, suggested that I have to be comfortable with whatever I bring becoming muddy. It's starting to sink in, what I agreed to do. Anyway, it's only three months. Twelve weeks will go by fast. Ninety days is nothing—it's between oil changes. I'll have to get my oil changed when I get back. No, can't start thinking of getting back. I'll miss my dog.

Next update: Amsterdam.

June 3, 2013

I'm halfway through with briefings. In between I'm meeting other MSFers who are either coming back from a mission or are also on their way out. By lunchtime I've already had two discussions about bombings, in two different settings. I'm reminded that the real "heroes" in the field are the national folks who remain in places where even MSF doesn't go. No one here wants to be thought of as a saint or an angel. They just want to get the work done, and done right.

The "specialness" of MSF wears off quick when talk of work starts. There's a job here that has to be done. I'm told of the nuances of the challenges on the field. I'm tasked to work myself out of a job. I've got three months to establish a sustainable monitoring system for everything on this mission. And I have to be ready to have no epidemiologist to whom I should hand it off.

I'm a little scared.

I suppose it's good that my last briefing is with the psychosocial care unit. I don't know how raw these emails are going to be, so let me introduce the disclaimer now: Please be advised. Mothers, feel free to censor. To my mother, I'm sorry in advance.

Next update: Juba.

June 4, 2013

Surprisingly, I made my connection in Nairobi. Turns out you really do only need an hour.

Fortunately, my bags made it too.

Sorry to say that I won't have any photos from Juba to show you. Photography is strictly forbidden. The "immigration" was in fact a mass of people pushed up against a wall of windows, hands in the air clutching passports, pink cards, and money. My passport disappeared for about 45 minutes and then I just had to wait. This will probably be the biggest lesson: learning that sometimes all you can do is wait.

That's what I'm doing now. I got my passport back and found the MSF driver to take me to the office. I've had my briefings here at the Juba office, and now I'm just waiting for a car to take me to the MSF house so I can take a shower and hopefully eat lunch.

That's all to report for now, but know I've landed safely and am scheduled to be on the MSF plane tomorrow (hopefully I'll get a snapshot of that from the field).

© Sandy Althomsons

June 6, 2013

Maban, Day 2

I don't even know where to begin. I intended to write a few short snippets whenever I could get on the internet, but it's only been 24 hours and I have so much to tell. I wish I could videotape my entire life here for y'all.

I can't believe I got off the plane 24 hours ago. That had to have been the best plane ride EVER. I sat right behind the pilot; I could have tapped him on the shoulder! I chatted with Nick, the copilot, the whole time. When we're at cruising altitude, they really have nothing to do, so we watched videos on their iPads. Of course, that stopped when the rains hit, and they "worked for their salaries." I've got video, but you'll have to wait 'til I get back as internet is quite slow here.

We stopped at Loki Choggio, Kenya, on the way. This used to be the logistics hub for all humanitarian work in Sudan. Now it's practically a ghost town. Nick was happy to show me the duty free store, but it was closed. Someone ran to get the store clerk, who came running to open a small room of mostly empty shelves. What there *was* was liquor. Still, he had good prices so I bought a bottle of vodka, figuring someone will drink it on the mission. It always helps to bring alcohol when making friends.

There were no goats or cows on the landing strip when we flew into Doro, but plenty of children watching. There were three white guys with MSF vests on, and Nick steered me towards them. One of them was headed out, but I traveled back with the other two.

© Sandy Althomsons

I was thrilled to learn I get my own tent. Turns out the epidemiologist sits on the coordination (management) team, which has its own separate compound and office space. This will only last until the end of the year, as they are turning this emergency mission into a regular mission.

Then the coordination team moves to Juba. Finally, I got my timing right! Still, the tent only had a twin mattress, stinky sheet, and a bed net with plenty of holes in it. I raided the empty tent across the way for a floor mat, chair, metal trunk, pillow, and better bed net, and now my tent feels like home. I even hung up a rosary my friend Melissa gave me so now my tent has the faint fragrance of rose.

Wednesday is pizza night. I'm amazed at what logs (logisticians) can do in the field. This pizza oven is something even Atlanta's Antico Pizza Napoletana would be impressed with. There were expats everywhere—about 40 people—from everywhere, even a cute Indian guy (score!). I didn't stay long though, as I felt the dirtiest and stinkiest I've ever felt.

The latrines are surprisingly clean and not stinky, though I guess they have to be this way to prevent hepatitis E. I think I missed the big wave, as numerous water and sanitation interventions were put in place two days before I got here. Whew, good timing again.

The showers aren't too bad either, though they require the type of coordination I used back in my college days: carrying shampoo and soap around while wrapped in a large towel.

Today I went around with the epidemiologist to a few of the camps. We even walked through the marketplace with two other expats. Donkeys and camels everywhere. There was even some dancing and singing as they were doing food distribution. One of the MSF expats jumped into the dancing circle. Surprisingly, I was too shy to join. I'm amazed at this marketplace. There is so much for sale—I don't know where this stuff comes from. Apparently the exchange rate is quite high. It's all the expats coming in to do humanitarian work and bringing dollars with them. Capitalism reigns supreme.

Tomorrow I really have to start working. I'll start with some data entry—though I have a data clerk, it's better to understand it from the ground up. Plus, it's easier to catch mistakes when you know the entire job. We work Saturdays too, so my weekend will start in two more days. They have barbeque instead of pizza on Saturdays. It's meant to boost morale. This mission has been coined the "burning" mission, because they burn through so many expats. Apparently a three-month mission is quite respectable here. And I have a shitload of work to do.

Oh, and Brian, my colleague back home whom I teased incessantly when he wore the same color combination as our administrative assistant, will be happy to hear that on my first day, Viktor, the log from Czech Republic, was wearing a blue and white striped T-shirt, just like me. He called me "sister" all night.

P.S. I read ALL your emails. They mean oh so much to me. Unfortunately I can't manage to send much, so apologies in advance for not replying, but please know I am reading them, and they warm my heart to know you are there reading mine.

June 9, 2013

Maban, Day 5

Yesterday I had already started to count the days, but today is a day of rest and I'm feeling better. I was hoping to do laundry, but the rains started last night, and they haven't yet stopped. At breakfast there was already a group going out to move the maternity ward from the clinic to the new hospital (keep in mind these are all tents). I guess I'll do some data cleaning at least. It's really hard to not work when everyone else is working, and there is really so much to do.

Photos © Jean-Pierre Amigo

I'm having crazy dreams. Must be the Lariam.

I'm getting into the work now, and it's really complicated. I'm a bit confused, but the current epidemiologist reassured me that after a week's cycle of reporting it would all make sense.

We drove past the camps yesterday on our way to one of the clinics. These people really have nothing. Still, when they smile, their whole faces light up. I tried to smile just as warmly but I was holding back tears. How can they smile through this?

In my briefing with the emergency coordinator, she explained how their homes had been bombed from the sky about 60 kilometers from these camps. I'm not sure why, mostly political reasons. Their resilience is beyond anything I could imagine.

I'm trying to learn Arabic by picking up words from those who know. I can count to ten. I really want to communicate with the population. It would be easy to stay in the office, hang out with expats, and never leave the compound. It would be really easy. But I want to know these people; these people with the strength to survive anything.

June 14, 2013

Maban, Day 10

10 days; feels like I just got here.

My hands perpetually smell like chlorine. I suppose that's good considering I've managed to stay healthy so far (touch wood).

They tell me the situation is getting better here. There are no more expats being medevaced (medical evacuation, I saw the last one leave when I arrived), the number of Hep E patients has dropped considerably since the peak in February–March, and there is a better cook in the canteen. Still, we are all bracing for the rains.

© Marcella Kraay

The rains came again two days ago. After four hours of perpetual downpour, my tent remained dry (whew). I met a Canadian nurse yesterday and she was initially worried about her tent, until she saw all the tents in the refugee camp. They all leak. She had no sympathy left for herself. It's like that here. No matter how primitive or miserable the setting may be, no one complains. We know we have it way better than the people we are serving.

I saw my first (and unfortunately probably not last) scorpion last night. Scared me more than the snake I discovered the week before. Our emco (emergency coordinator, AKA "the big boss") killed the snake with a rock. She's a badass. I'm a chickenshit and diligently zip up my tent every morning and night and shake out my shoes and bedding regularly.

I'm looking forward to Sunday's day off, though on Monday we start a measles vaccine campaign. I'm helping out with the monitoring. I'm also doing data collection with the outreach teams, as well as the regular Hep E and mortality surveillance. There is no shortage of work to be done.

Still, I'm dreaming of lying around somewhere on Sunday morning and reading this Dan Brown novel I brought with me. It'll be a relief to just stop thinking for a while.

June 19, 2013

Maban, Days 14, 15, & 16 (Yesterday, today, and tomorrow)

Yesterday: It rained last night, and the snakes and scorpions came out again. My count is up to three snakes and three scorpions. I found one in my bed four nights ago.

Surprisingly, I'm getting comfortable now. It's taken about two weeks, but yesterday was the first day that I thought I could actually make it through all three months. It's stressful living in this heightened state of alertness. I notice everything that moves. I can tell the difference between a grasshopper and a lizard outside my tent just by the noise it makes. But it's hard to slow down when everyone else is working so hard. We all think in six-week chunks. At six weeks, we are sent for a weekend of R&R in Loki Choggio. Two weeks down, four to go.

Today: We are in the midst of a measles vaccination campaign. I had no idea what I was doing on Monday. Today is Wednesday and I'm an expert. At the end of each day, I'm the most popular person on the mission.

Four days ago I trained 30 Arabic-speaking daily workers on how to tally measles vaccinations in a mass campaign. At 5:00PM, as all my tally sheets float in, everyone comes looking for me. They don't have to say anything; they all have the same look with big eyes and wide smiles. Yes, I nod and grin, we exceeded expectations again. We're expected to vaccinate 19,000 children by Friday; we're at 17,500 on Wednesday. Vaccination campaigns are a surefire way to boost morale amongst humanitarian workers. Immediate gratification.

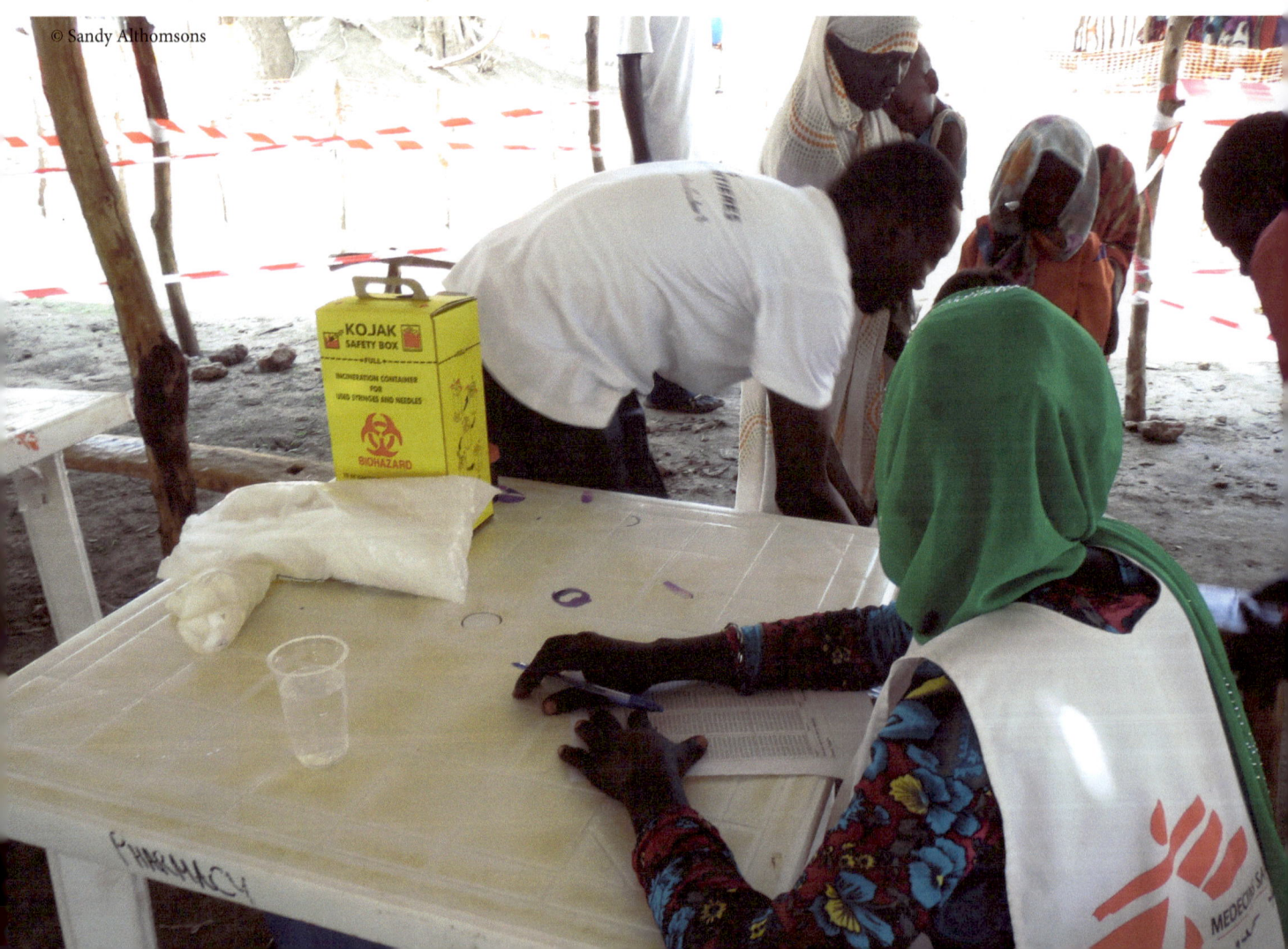

© Sandy Althomsons

Tomorrow: Tomorrow is World Refugee Day. If you think of me, please think of the 42 million displaced people on this planet. I know it's just a statistic, so keep this in mind: we expats here in Maban County, South Sudan, count the days until our end of mission. We are just visitors into the life of a refugee. Their courage, strength, and joy are beyond anything I can conceive.

Yes, they survived bombs dropped on their homes and the 60 kilometer trek through treacherous land, and live in the most meager living standards established for them in these camps, but their smiles will make you weep. The children cry out "Kawaja! Kawaja! Kawaja!" (non-African) after all white land cruisers driving by, waving their hands and grinning ear to ear, looking for that connection—the returned smile and wave. I am grateful for any part of their life they are willing to share with me.

© Jean-Pierre Amigo

June 23, 2013

Maban, Day 19

There are all kinds of characters on this mission. Workaholics, alcoholics, constant givers, attention seekers, problem solvers, egomaniacs, adrenaline junkies, kind hearts, badasses, chickenshits, sexaholics, and commitmentphobes. But everyone is dedicated and no one is lazy. Except on Sundays.

I start my Sundays with laundry, just to get it over with. The best you can hope for when doing laundry in South Sudan is "clean enough." Some people are happy if soap just touches their clothes. Walk through our camp today and you'll see MSF T-shirts waving on clothes lines, like flags marking a holiday.

I killed my first scorpion last night, without even flinching. I found it just outside my tent, picked up a rock, and crushed it, then left it there as a warning to others. I have two spider bites on my right arm. I think they're going to leave scars—my South Sudan tattoo. Interestingly, I've become less anxious and more comfortable with every unpleasant event. I'm not sure why living through difficulties makes life seem easier. I feel like I can survive anything after this. But it's still damn hot.

I'm going to find a shady spot with a breeze and read a few more chapters of my Dan Brown novel. In between I'll be dreaming of all the ripe peaches and blueberries on my parents' farm just waiting to be picked. Wishing you all a lovely Sunday, and a happy, happy birthday to my big brother!

June 26, 2013

Maban, Day 22

Yesterday, *the* medco arrived here in the field. He is the head medical coordinator for all MSF-Holland missions in South Sudan. My boss, medco for just the Maban mission, asked ME to give *the* medco a briefing on the hepatitis E situation. WTF?! I've been here for three weeks and now I'm the Hep E expert?

Here's what I know: Hepatitis E is typically transmitted in refugee camps through fecal-contaminated drinking water. Even if a clean water source is provided, jerry cans and hands can become unhygienic in the household, contaminating the water. The virus attacks the liver, rendering it debilitated and unable to filter the toxins that enter the body. The result is an acute infection that presents with jaundice—yellow eyes—from which people usually recover. But it can be fatal, especially for pregnant women. We have no cure, vaccine, or treatment for hepatitis E. All we can offer is palliative care.

In February and March, the hepatitis E outbreak reached its peak in the refugee camps of Maban and many people died in the MSF clinic. The clinic got a bad reputation, as did the MSF cars that transported the ailing patients and the MSF kawaja health staff who worked there. It's been challenging to regain the trust of the population.

MSF has clinics in four camps in Maban, and I'm collecting data for three of them. With the rainy season upon us, we are expecting additional cases. There is already a spike in one of the camps, though I suspect it's due to active case-finding by the outreach teams actively looking for cases instead of patients passively presenting to clinics with symptoms. I'm trying to be creative in assessing the situation, but even after three weeks I feel like I don't know enough. Still, I've made a plan to identify those who are at greatest risk of death, or even hospitalization. Perhaps if we can target the most vulnerable population, we can at least keep the case fatality rate low. It's nerve-wracking to feel so inadequate in such a crisis situation.

June 30, 2013

Maban, Day 26

I had one of those "What the F am I doing here?" moments today, but it only lasted about two hours. It started when I got up from reading my book and had to go to the bathroom. I thought, "Ugh, I have to pee in a latrine again. This is never going to end."

I think my mental state might have had something to do with the headache I had, which also might have had something to do with the vodka I drank last night. There is little sympathy in the field for self-inflicted pain.

Yesterday I went to the hospital, just to check it out. I'm not sure what I was expecting, but it's a collection of galvanized steel huts and tents—very basic standards. There's a pediatric ward, an ER, an outpatient department, and even a therapeutic feeding center for malnourished children.

While I was standing outside the maternity tent, a Pajero SUV rushed in and two bodies were dumped to the ground. The men were groaning and bleeding from their heads. They'd had a fight, but clearly with some metal objects. There were no translators around, so I still don't know if the tension was between refugees, refugees and the local population, or just the local population. MSF doesn't really care; a patient is a patient.

My colleagues grabbed their gloves and a couple orange stretchers and rushed into action. After the patients were stabilized and sent via Land Cruisers to the hospital 45 minutes away (the only one with a surgeon), a little boy came in with his mother, gripping an injured hand. He had a nine-day-old snakebite that had become septic. I just stood there and watched.

Half of my brain wishes I was a stronger person, like Helle, the Danish outreach nurse. The other half wishes I didn't care so much and could just go home. I suppose it's normal to want to let go a little. Somehow having a drink seemed like a better idea last night. For some folks here, drinking is a real coping mechanism. I don't fault anyone for their crutches. We all have our own. The emails you send are lifelines for me. Your words of encouragement help recover my diminishing fortitude. Some have noted the uniqueness of MSFers here on mission— that there are few people willing to do so much to help those in need. But we question our decisions daily, and rarely feel like we're doing enough. There is no shortage of humility here.

© Sandy Althomsons

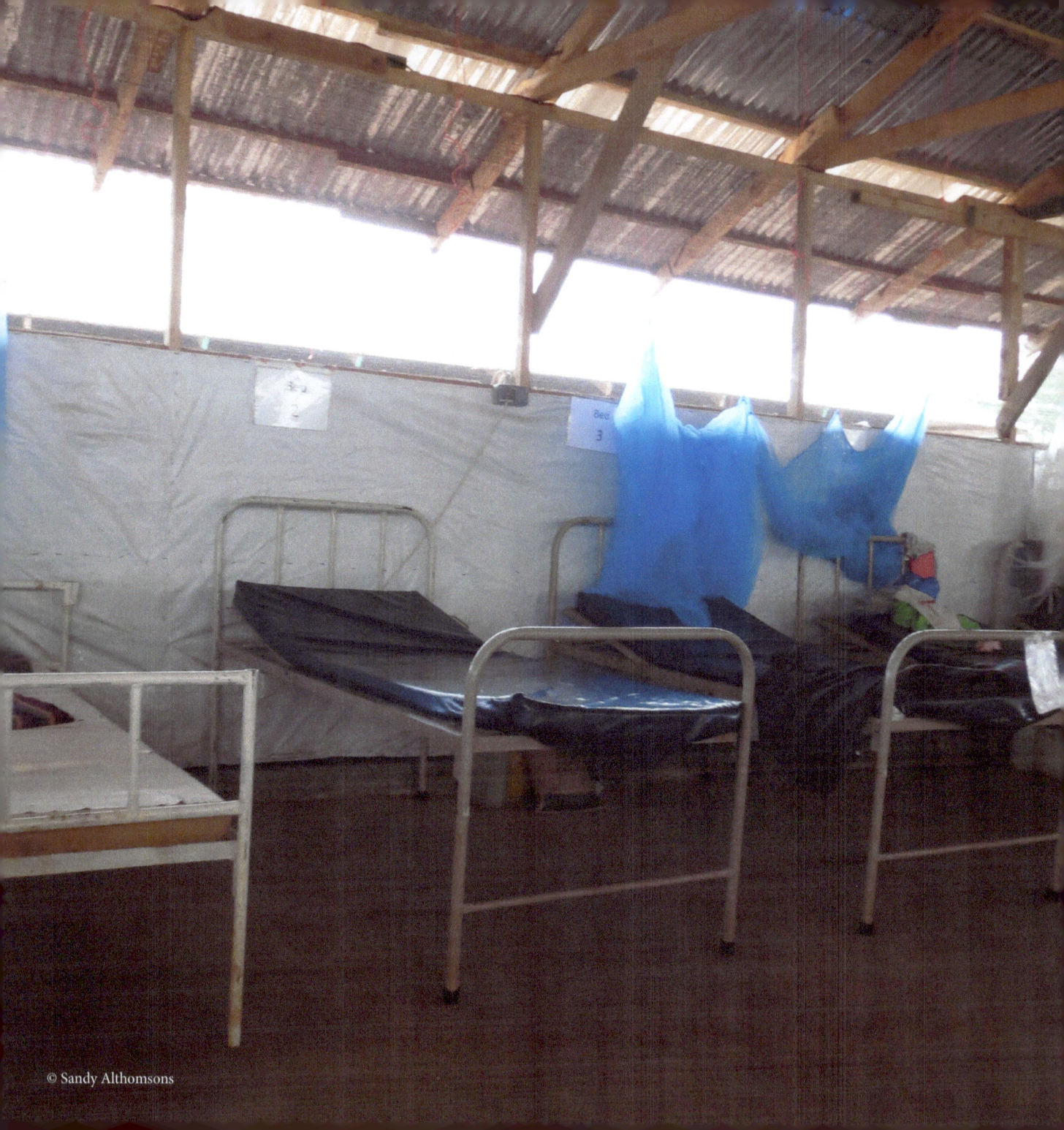

July 5, 2013

Maban, Day 31

I think I've found my rhythm.

I went out with the outreach workers today, just to get a sense of where all the data is coming from. My "body guard" was Said, a Darfurian who was raised in the Blue Nile state of Sudan but is now a refugee with the rest of the Ingessana population that is here. We were looking for malnourished children and sick people, encouraging them to seek help at the feeding centers and clinics. We gave people who couldn't walk a slip of paper with a drawing of a donkey head. They were instructed to get someone to present this paper to the donkey "ambulance" to get them to the OPD (outpatient department).

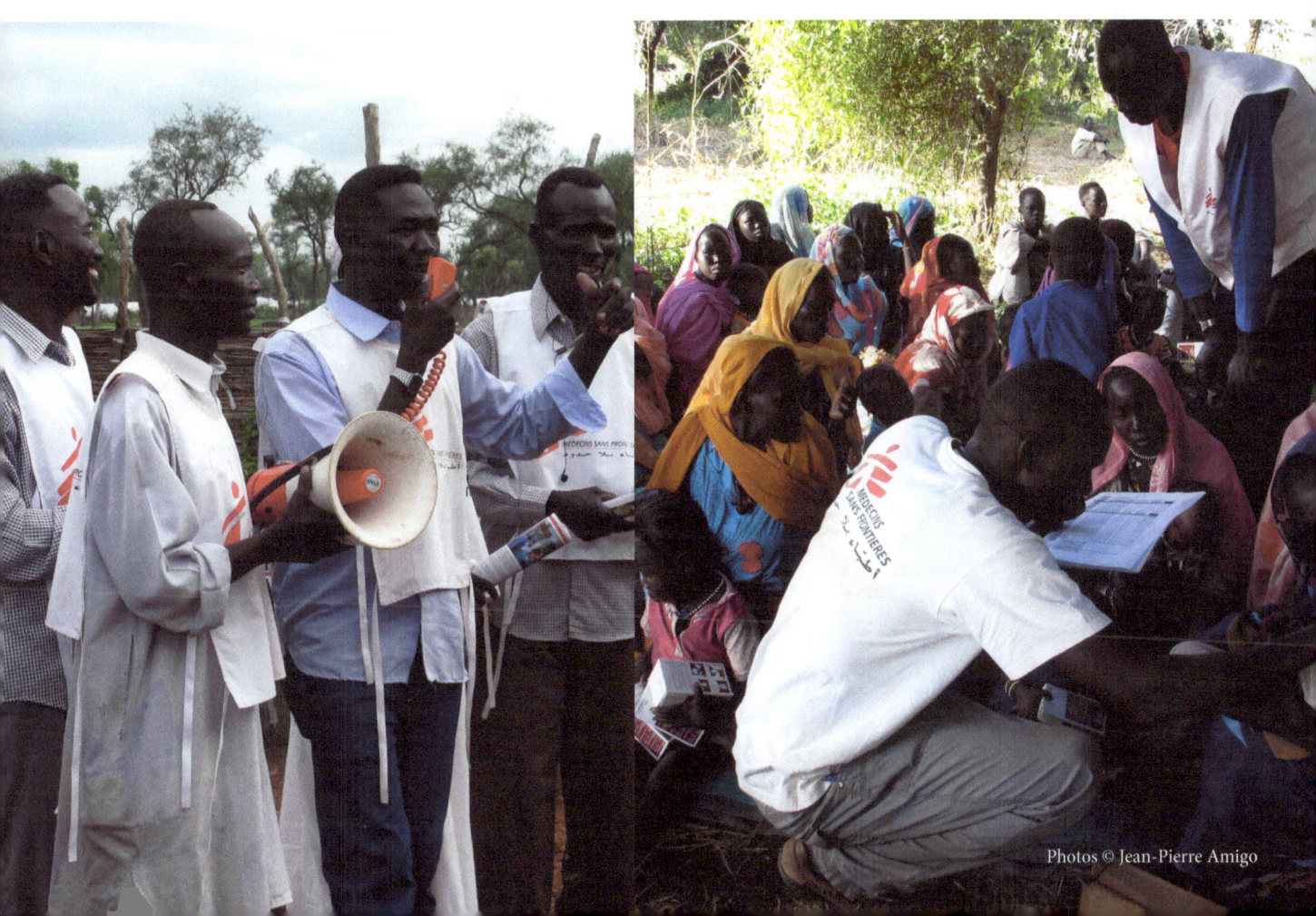

Photos © Jean-Pierre Amigo

It's an understatement to say these people have nothing. Their tents are propped up in the mud (which will become a swamp when the rains start) and they make fences from the prickly branches of the local trees. But they have the widest smiles and the brightest, whitest, straightest teeth. They are really beautiful people.

© Jean-Pierre Amigo

I missed the US Independence Day celebrations; Tuesday (July 9) will be South Sudan's Independence Day. Our national staff has the day off. Expats still have to work. I'm getting a little worn out with the nonstop 80-hour work week, but there are light-hearted moments that keep the rhythm going.

Last night we had a spontaneous "party" with a bottle of Amarula, some chocolates from Juba, and a bag of gummy bears that I had forgotten about in the fridge. Gummy bears are like crack here. Even the tough logisticians soften with a handful of gummy bears. Deprivation breeds appreciation.

I stopped counting the days to the end of my mission. Today I actually thought I might miss this place when I return home. I told this to Marcus, our Austrian PC (project coordinator), and he explained it from the perspective of a Sherpa of the Himalayas. They trek up Mount Everest as guides and at times abruptly stop and rest. When questioned why they were stopping, they simply explained that they were waiting for their souls to catch up. I think mine caught up to me today.

July 12, 2013

Maban, Day 38

The head of mission arrived here in the field yesterday and I had a 10-minute conversation with him. It changed my perspective completely. I now realize that the medical team here might not know how to use an epidemiologist. This makes my job even harder, but it also means that I have a lot of freedom to work. This is MSF—find your way.

I keep thinking I have reached my lowest threshold for being dirty, and then another day happens. I spent Wednesday night at our Kaya camp to participate in Robert's farewell party. He's a Kenyan nurse supervisor—he'd been here one year! The next morning, after a night of barbeque fumes and dance-sweat infused into my t-shirt, all I had left to wear was my pajama shirt. I arrived back at our base camp (Batil) to a day of nonstop rain. I didn't make it to the shower until the next morning.

I don't mind cold showers anymore, I'll eat anything you put in front of me, and I prefer the squat latrines. I think I've become a bit feral. I hope I remember to flush when I return home.

I had to say goodbye to Helle today. She's our Danish outreach nurse who commands more than 70 outreach workers, who are all refugees themselves. Her two supervisors speak a bit of English, but few on the team are literate in Arabic. She is utterly devoted to the refugee population, but will tell them to "get in the fucking truck" when her staff are just milling about. She is my hero, and a force that will be missed.

July 18, 2013

Maban, Day 44

I'm spending more of my time analyzing the data, looking for gaps in treatment. I need to get back out into the community to understand it better. I want to be a real "shoe-leather" epidemiologist while I can.

Tomorrow I leave for R&R in the MSF compound at Loki Choggio. I've heard that one of the earliest human fossils was found near there. I've also heard there is a cliff about 100 meters from the compound that was the inspiration for the setting in the Lion King. I've also heard there is ice cream.

Hopefully I'll have access to the internet and can reply to your emails. I really enjoy hearing news from home. Yesterday I got a string of emails from my home owners association discussing a water break in my neighborhood—one person even asked what she would do for water. Third world problems become first world problems.

July 24, 2013

Maban, Day 50

I am impressed by how many family and friends have South Sudan in their newsfeed. Here's what I know: The president of South Sudan sacked his cabinet, including the vice-president. This is ahead of an anticipated oil shutdown. The largest revenue stream for South Sudan comes from its oil production, particularly here in Upper Nile state. But so far the only pipeline out is through Sudan.

How does this affect us? I'm not sure it will (out here in the bush), though it might indirectly. MSF has been in South Sudan for over 20 years. We think that maybe our flights into and out of Juba could be affected; for now we're just waiting and seeing. But further down the line, when South Sudan's revenues decline and there is less of a pie to go around, you can be sure the least of the least will be at the end of the line. Priorities.

July 31, 2013

Maban, Day 57

It's a good day. I woke up to pink and white balloons in my office and a big sign outside my door. I was promptly greeted at breakfast with hugs from everyone. I even got some presents: soap and gummy bears! Very cherished items.

Our cook just returned from a holiday, so we had boiled eggs and Dutch pancakes for breakfast. :)

I spent the morning introducing a proposed nutritional survey to one of our outreach teams, then later explained to one of our clinical officers why we need to keep a close eye on a population in one of the camps that is potentially susceptible to hepatitis E. I spent this afternoon finalizing my weekly mortality and morbidity reports, as well as projecting how many cases of malaria we can expect next month. I feel accomplished.

Now I'm going to have a shower and put on a dress. Wednesdays are pizza party nights. I might even break out the dangling earrings and some lipstick. This year I timed my birthday perfectly.

P.S. Thanks for all the wishes sent my way!! The internet is acting up so I can't respond to all today, but know that I read them!!

August 7, 2013

Maban, Day 64

I put on sunscreen every morning like it's war paint. My biggest decision in the morning is sweaty feet (Gumboots) or itchy feet (sandals that let mosquitoes bite). The greatest skill in MSF is flexibility, so when the government announced a four-day weekend for the end of Ramadan (Eid el Fitr), we simply accommodated accordingly.

I have a few weeks left of my three-month mission. I know the pace of life continues back home, but I suspect I'll be like the girl who crawled out of the wardrobe after living a lifetime in Narnia.

I will spend the rest of my time here conducting a nutritional survey in one of the camps. I have to train a team of twelve people, of whom only two speak some English. Maybe half are literate in Arabic.

I am comfortable in uncertainty.

In other news: Nairobi's international terminal burned down today. Fortunately I had just rerouted my outward bound flight through Addis Ababa.

© Sandy Althomsons

August 15, 2013

Maban, Day 72

There's really too much to tell in these short emails.

I spent the afternoon with the outreach team walking through one of the refugee camps (there are four here). We found a few patients to refer to our clinic. One was an older man who was feeling pain in his leg. When we found him, he had placed a tourniquet on himself and had cut his leg multiple times. He was bleeding out the "bad blood" into a hole he had dug in the ground. He said he had done this before. Though he agreed to go to the clinic, he simply untied his tourniquet, covered up the hole with dirt, then proceeded to wipe ash on his cuts. I was trying to ascertain his age, and for a split second I thought to myself that whatever he's been doing has kept him in good health so far.

MSF has been in South Sudan for over 20 years. It's good MSF is here, providing care to those who need it. Perhaps the hardest part is figuring out who needs it.

MSF has also been in Somalia for over 20 years, but recently announced that they are leaving. Since 1991, 16 MSF workers have been killed there. I wonder what will happen to the people there who need health services. I also wonder what it takes for a population to get the government they deserve.

Cairo is on fire.

I should be counting down the days, but I'm not. I've planned a mini-excursion to Ethiopia before my return home because I just don't think I can jump back into the minutiae of daily life in America. I hope my friends and colleagues will be patient with my re-acclimation.

August 22, 2013

Maban, Day 79

One week left in Maban. I'm down to my last Thursday, Friday, Saturday, Sunday, Monday, Tuesday, and Wednesday. Every day I'll remind everyone which day it is. That's how it's done here.

We are concluding our nutritional survey. Having the opportunity to walk through the camp and interact with people getting on with their daily lives was a gift. Watching fathers and mothers laugh as their children screamed in fear at the kawaja (me) was disconcerting. Now I'm in panic mode to finish the report.

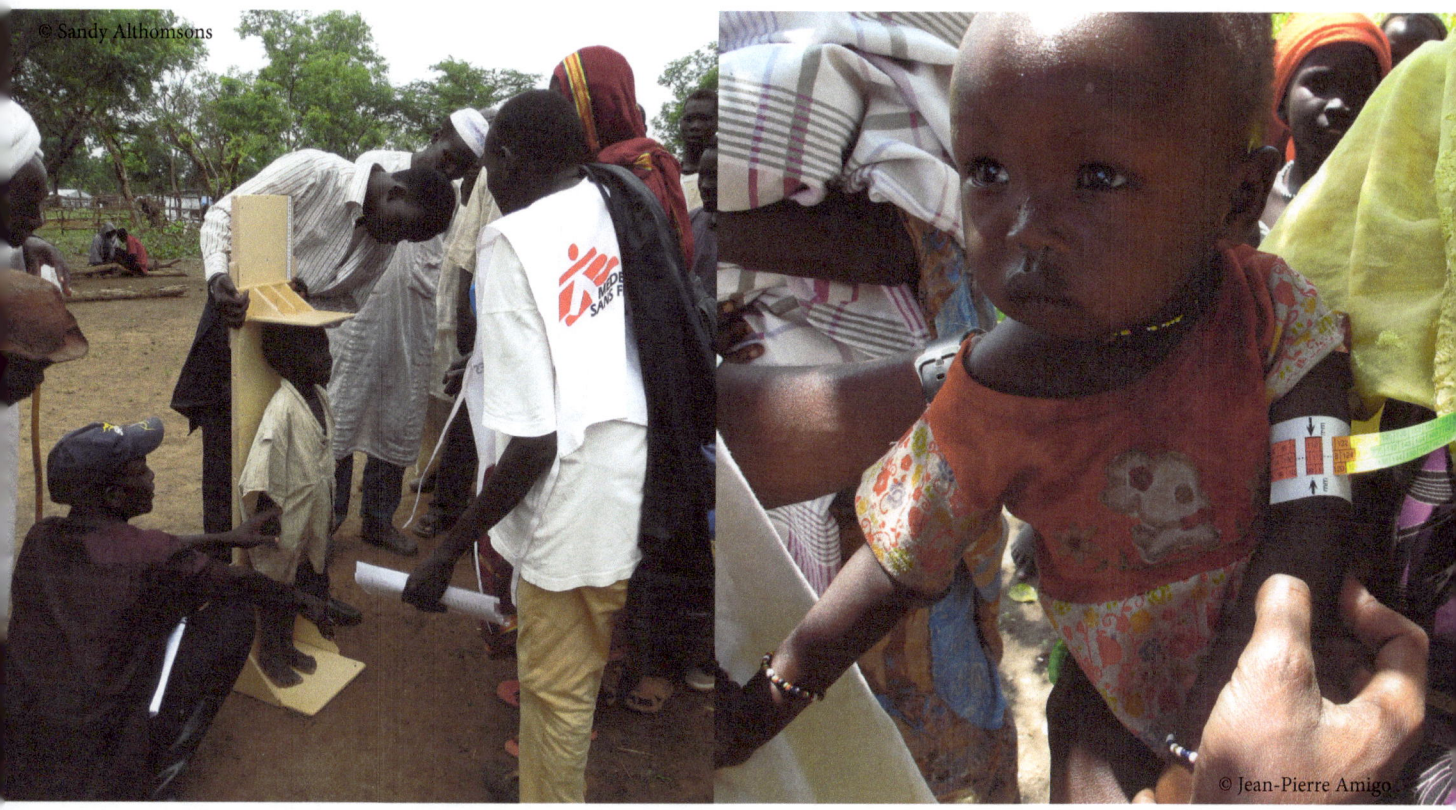

I don't have many descriptions left, mostly thoughts. Lots of thoughts.

I know I'm fortunate to have had the chance to experience what I've experienced. I'm also lucky to have friends, colleagues, and family who are interested in what I'm doing and send me constant words of encouragement. "Thank you" can never be enough. I hope I have the strength and patience to not become an arrogant humanitarian aid worker who thinks she has done her part to save the world.

The world doesn't need saving.

But it could use a little more understanding.

So thanks for sharing in my understanding of these three months in South Sudan.

August 29, 2013

Maban, Day 86

Security is the most important thing in an MSF mission. We constantly radio our movements to the base so our location is always known. Each refugee camp's name has a code based on the radio alphabet. Batil is Bravo Alpha. Kaya is Kilo Yankee. Gendrassa is Gulf Delta. Doro (the airstrip) is Delta Oscar.

We always announce the number of passengers (plus one driver) in the car. When reporting our current status as okay, we say "everything Oscar Kilo." This constant radio chatter has been the soundtrack of my life in South Sudan. I will miss hearing my friends' voices over the air waves; it was always reassuring.

I leave Maban today and tomorrow will leave South Sudan for Ethiopia. Final destination: Atlanta.

Mobile 42: "Bravo Alpha for mobile four-two."

Batil: "Four-two, go ahead."

Mobile 42: "Leaving your location for Delta Oscar, four plus one on board. Over."

Batil: "Good copy. Safe journey. Over."

Mobile 42: "Thanks, over and out."

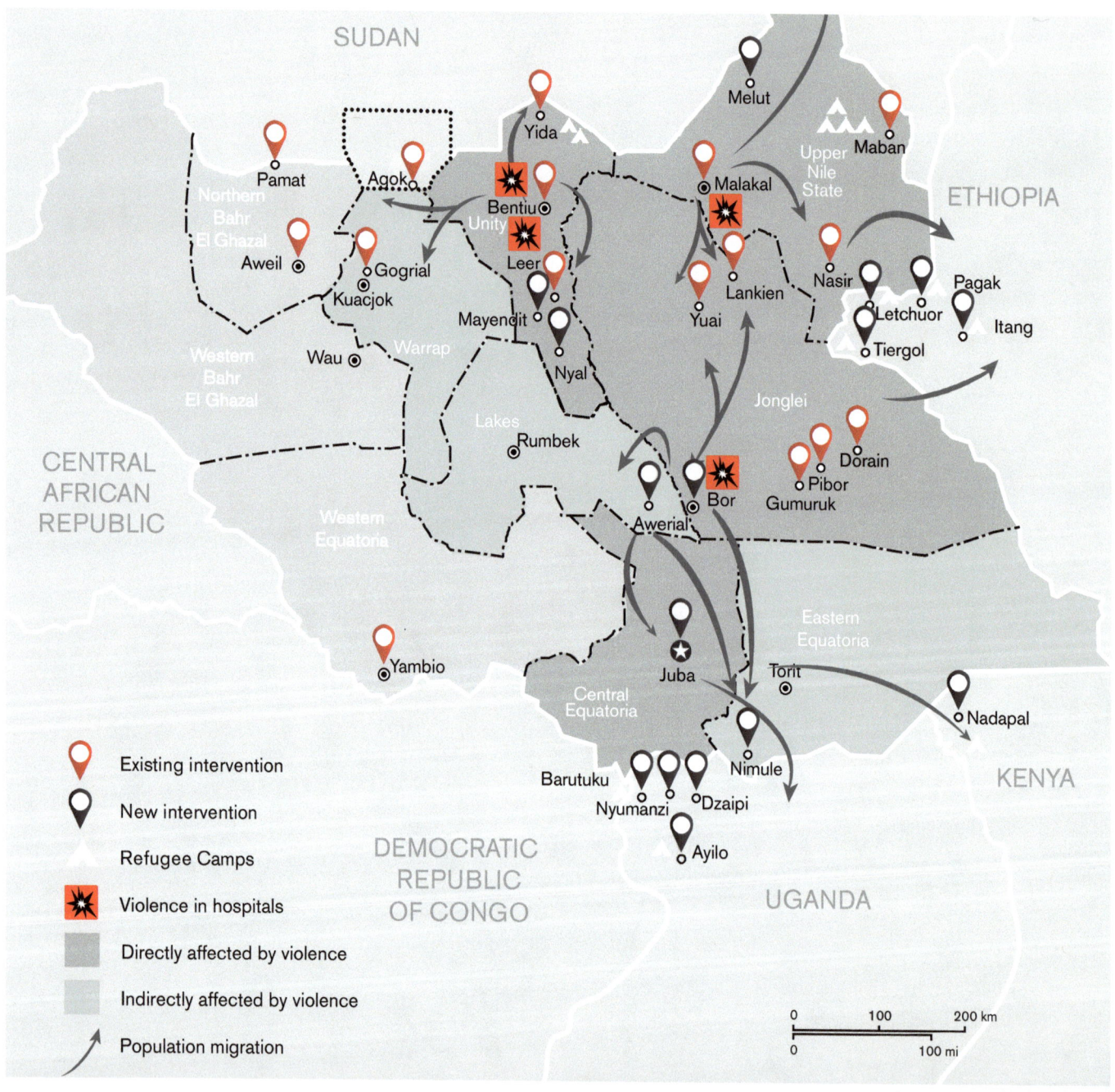

Epilogue

Doctors Without Borders/Médecins Sans Frontières (MSF) has more than 3,800 international and local staff in South Sudan responding to the humanitarian crisis, supported by 62 international staff providing operational assistance from neighbouring countries.

As of August 2014, MSF operates 26 projects in nine out of the ten states of South Sudan, including Unity, Upper Nile, and Jonglei state, where conflict has taken some of the heaviest tolls on the population. Teams are responding to various health needs including surgery, obstetrics, malaria, kala azar, cholera, vaccinations against preventable diseases, and malnutrition.

In Upper Nile state's Maban county, 122,000 refugees are sheltering after having fled the ongoing conflict in Sudan's Blue Nile state. MSF teams continue to provide primary and secondary healthcare in Doro camp, inpatient care in Batil camp and an emergency room in Kaya camp. MSF's teams also conduct outreach activities and operate mobile clinics in and around the three camps to provide health care and monitor the health situation of the refugee and host populations.

MSF also supports the public hospital in Bunj, providing primary healthcare and general vaccinations. The team has constructed cholera treatment units in Kaya and Gentil hospitals to bolster its preparedness in case of a cholera outbreak.

About the Author

Sandy Althomsons has been an epidemiologist with MSF since 2008 and has worked in Malawi, Uzbekistan, and South Sudan. She is a graduate of the Johns Hopkins School of Public Health, and when not on mission, works at the Centers for Disease Control and Prevention.

www.ingramcontent.com/pod-product-compliance
Lightning Source LLC
Chambersburg PA
CBHW042142290426
44110CB00002B/88